D0786266

Editor: PENNY CLARKE
Artists: MARK BERGIN
JOHN JAMES
GERALD WOOD

Produced by
THE SALARIYA BOOK CO. LTD
25 Marlborough Place
Brighton BN1 5UB
England

Published in the United States in 1999
by Peter Bedrick Books
A division of NTC/Contemporary
Publishing Group, Inc.
4255 West Touhy Avenue,
Lincolnwood (Chicago), Illinois
60646-1975 U.S.A.

Published by agreement with
Macdonald Young Books Ltd, England

Library of Congress Cataloging-in-Publication
Data

Macdonald, Fiona.
    First facts about the ancient Romans / written by Fiona
Macdonald : created and designed by David Salariya.
        p.   cm.
    Includes index.
    Summary: Presents in text and illustrations the history,
government, people, culture, and day-to-day life in ancient
Rome.
    ISBN 0-87226-496-3
    1. Rome--Juvenile literature.   [1. Rome--Civilization.]
I. Salariya, David.   II. Title.
DG77.M   1996
937.6--dc20   96-13269
                                         CIP
                                         AC

Printed in Hong Kong by
Wing King Tong

International Standard Book Number:
0-87226-496-3

99 00 01 02 03 15 14 13 12 11 10 9 8 7 6 5 4 3

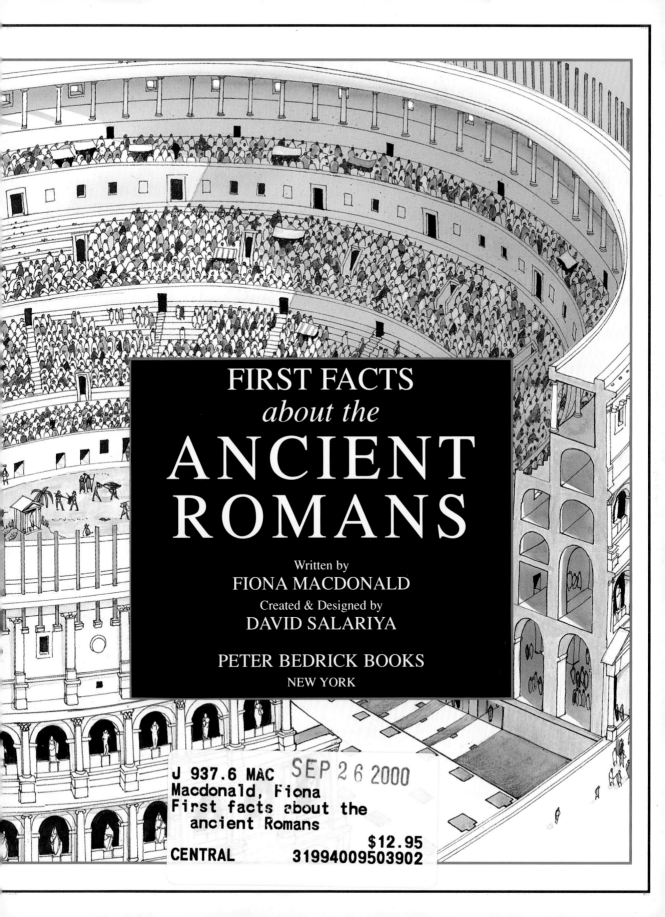

FIRST FACTS
about the
ANCIENT
ROMANS

Written by
FIONA MACDONALD

Created & Designed by
DAVID SALARIYA

PETER BEDRICK BOOKS
NEW YORK

CONTENTS

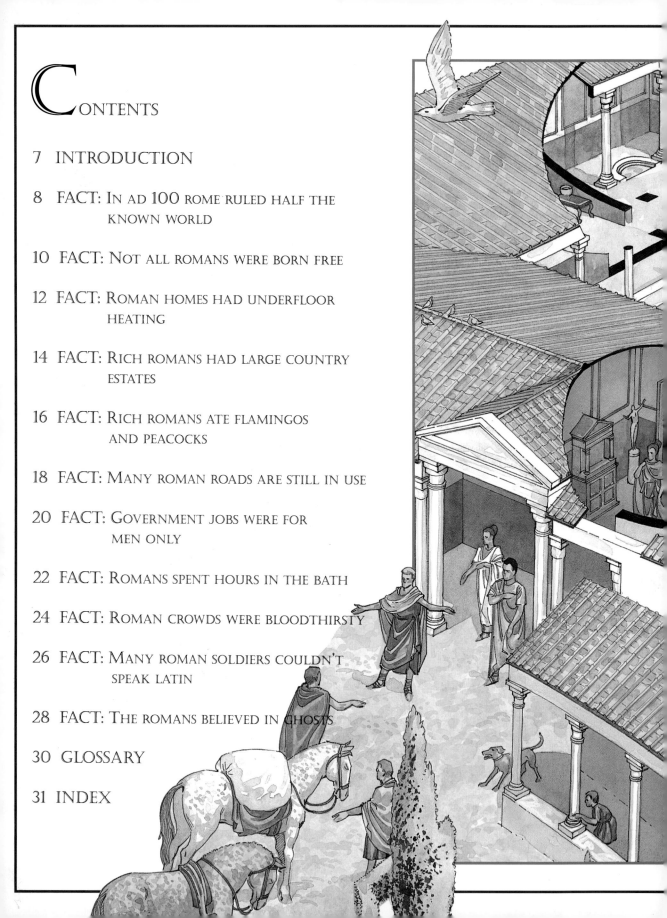

INTRODUCTION

THE ANCIENT ROMANS lived in Italy over two thousand years ago. They ruled one of the largest empires the Western world had known.

Those simple facts are true, but they do not convey the richness, or the enormous contrasts, of Roman civilization. Over the centuries, the Romans transformed their original cluster of villages into a magnificent city of a million people. It had fine buildings and efficient drains and sewers. Yet thousands of Romans lived in dingy slums with shaky walls and leaking roofs.

The Romans spent vast amounts of state money and private wealth on works of art. Their mosaics and sculptures are among the best in the world. Yet the streets around the fine buildings and statues were full of mud and rubbish, clogged with traffic, and the haunt of muggers and thieves.

The Romans were great law-makers, clever philosophers, excellent administrators and brilliant engineers. Their poets wrote heroic epics, wistful love lyrics and rude songs. For fun, Roman crowds liked to watch gladiators torture terrified prisoners and kill helpless wild animals. Roman rulers could be wickedly corrupt or prepared to die for noble ideals. Establishing the Roman Empire was a tremendous achievement, but it was won, and kept, through greed, brutality and fear.

FACT: IN AD 100 ROME RULED HALF THE KNOWN WORLD

THE FIRST ROMANS were farmers, living in small villages on seven neighboring hills. They flourished and prospered, and, by 753 BC, had founded the city of Rome.

After around 270 BC, Roman soldiers began to conquer nearby lands. By 30 BC, they ruled most of the countries bordering the Mediterranean Sea. In the 1st century AD they marched north to conquer Britain, Germany and France, and soon after AD 100 had conquered most of the Middle East, too.

The Roman Empire grew rich from taxes collected from conquered peoples, and also through trade. Essential food, especially corn, and many valuable luxury goods were shipped to Rome from distant lands, and sold to rich citizens in the city's shops and markets.

Roman power finally collapsed in AD 476.

AT ITS most powerful, the Roman Empire stretched from Scotland to the shores of the Black Sea.

Roman Empire Facts:

By AD 100 there were 60 million people living in the Roman Empire.

Everyone in the empire was governed by Roman laws.

Our word 'civilization' comes from 'civitas', the Roman word for city. Romans believed that cities were where the best-educated and most elegant people lived. They thought country people were slow-witted.

Conquered peoples resented Roman rule. As a British chieftain said, 'They make a wasteland, and call it peace.'

GERMANY

BRITAIN

FRANCE

Atlantic Ocean

SPAIN

THE ROMANS believed their empire brought good government to conquered lands. They appointed governors to rule conquered provinces, to collect taxes and make regular reports back to Rome.

IN THE 4th and 5th centuries AD, the Roman Empire was threatened by invasions of warlike tribes, the Huns, Vandals and Goths, who rode from the steppes of Central Asia to attack the empire's eastern frontier.

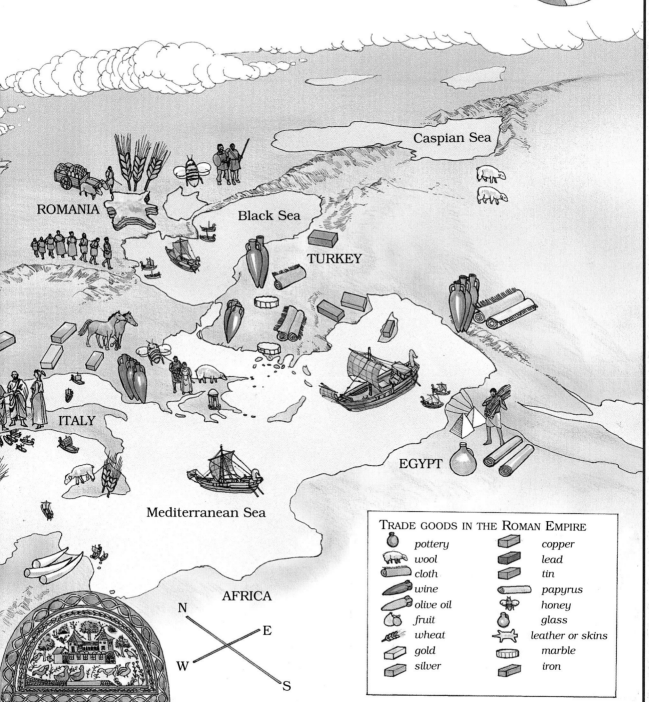

Caspian Sea

ROMANIA

Black Sea

TURKEY

ITALY

EGYPT

Mediterranean Sea

AFRICA

N

E

W

S

TRADE GOODS IN THE ROMAN EMPIRE

pottery		copper
wool		lead
cloth		tin
wine		papyrus
olive oil		honey
fruit		glass
wheat		leather or skins
gold		marble
silver		iron

9

FACT: NOT ALL ROMANS WERE BORN FREE

MORE THAN A MILLION PEOPLE lived in Rome in AD 100. But they were not all free-born citizens. Some were foreign merchants, some were peoples from the empire and very many were slaves. Roman law allowed anyone to come and live in the city, so long as they could support themselves. But they did not have full citizen's rights.

'Proper' Roman citizens belonged to one of three classes: patricians (nobles), equites (middle-rank) or plebs, short for plebeians (ordinary people).

Slaves might be prisoners, captured in war or purchased from slave-dealers in nearby lands. Others, the children of slaves, were born unfree.

SLAVES did all the dirty jobs their owners would not dream of doing.

EQUITES (middle-rank) families ran businesses, and owned property in Rome.

PATRICIANS were rich. They owned great country estates. Men from patrician families were appointed to all the top government jobs.

the patrician family's six household slaves (many more worked on the family's estate)

IT WAS a patrician wife's first duty to provide a son to inherit her husband's lands. Marriages were often arranged, to make alliances between noble, powerful families.

patrician couple with their three children and family pets

FARMERS brought food to sell in Rome's markets. Finding enough food to feed the citizens was often a problem for the government.

THERE were over 150 different trades in Rome, from wine merchants and goldsmiths to wagon-drivers and bakers. There were also many family-run shops and inns. The poorest citizens, who could only find part-time work, relied on government aid to survive.

MANY SLAVES worked as cooks, teachers, doctors and scribes. Some, freed by their owners, became rich.

Facts about Roman People:
Roman fathers had the power of life and death over their children and their slaves.

Citizens had many privileges. Only citizens could go to the public baths, attend gladiatorial games or receive free food from the government.

In AD 212, Emperor Caracalla made all free-born inhabitants of the empire full citizens of Rome.

WOMEN from 'respectable' families did not take part in public life. But at home they would discuss politics with their husbands, and influence them.

FACT: ROMAN HOMES HAD UNDERFLOOR HEATING

THE RICHEST ROMANS lived in grand style. They had comfortable houses set in beautiful gardens, hidden from the rest of the city behind high walls.

Not all Roman homes were as pleasant as this. By the 1st century AD, building land in Rome was scarce and expensive. To make maximum use of space, Roman architects designed 'insulae' (islands) – blocks of apartments, sometimes six stories high. Ordinary families lived there, crammed into one or two rented rooms. These blocks were badly built, noisy, dirty and dangerous – some fell down and others caught fire.

THE TEMPLE of Jupiter Capitoline, Rome's special god, dominated the surrounding streets.

INSULAE had flat or clay-tiled roofs. The top-floor attic rooms were the cheapest. There were shops at street level.

Facts about Roman Homes:
Roman drinking water pipes were made of lead – a slow poison that can cause infertility, brain damage in young children and loss of the sense of taste.

Fire was a serious hazard. There was a fire brigade, staffed by slaves. They were issued with axes, buckets and leather hosepipes to help them fight fires. After six years' service, fire-fighters were rewarded by being made Roman citizens.

MANY BLOCKS of flats had central courtyards to provide light and fresh air. Often, there was a communal lavatory in the courtyard. If not, tenants used public lavatories on street corners, or kept big pottery jars in their rooms. Fullers (who processed woolen cloth) paid to collect stale urine from lavatories. They used it to help dye cloth.

THE WEALTHY had homes with under-floor heating, using hot air from a wood-burning furnace in the cellar.

ONLY wealthy Romans could afford the space for courtyards and fountains in their homes in the middle of the city.

ELEGANT furniture (above) for a rich patrician's home was made of wood inlaid with ivory, silver and gold.

FLOORS were raised on low pillars. The hot air circulated beneath, so warming the floor.

URINAL (man's portable toilet) made of terracotta.

MAKERS of mosaic floors used lime-stone for white and blue, brick for red and purple, and glass gave other colors.

1 OIL LAMP on low stand. 2 Lamp stand. 3 Charcoal burner for heating rooms.

LAMPS burned oil made from olives, nuts, fish or seeds. They gave a golden light.

DOORS were made of wood, with lattices to let in cooling summer breezes.

WALLS of rich peoples' houses were decorated with beautiful paintings.

LAYING a mosaic floor – with patterns of tiny cubes of stone and glass.

FACT: RICH ROMANS HAD LARGE COUNTRY ESTATES

IN MANY PARTS of the empire there were vast estates owned by patrician families. Each estate was centered around a grand villa (country house), where the owner and his family stayed in the hot summers, or whenever they wanted to get away from Rome.

The estate farms were used to raise animals and grow crops: wheat and barley (for bread), olives (for oil) and grapes (to make wine). There were orchards and vegetable gardens, too. Some of this produce was for the family; the rest was for sale. Farming was big business in Roman times.

MANY VILLAS had beautiful gardens and shady colonnades, where the family could walk out of the glare of the sun. Many villa gardens were decorated with stone statues.

VILLAS had many rooms: for living, entertaining, reading, dining, sleeping, washing and cooking. The slaves' quarters were separate, but close to the villa.

OLIVES were crushed in a huge press. The oil they produced was stored in pottery jars buried in the ground to keep cool. Grain was ground in a horse-powered mill to make flour.

pigsties

Facts about Country Life:

Poor peasant families worked on their own small farms. On big estates, most work was done by slaves. Rich men owned hundreds.

Wealthy patrician families gained most of their income from farming.

Country people believed that every place had a guardian spirit. Rivers, rocks and trees were home to spirits, too.

VINES were pruned in winter to make them give good crops next autumn. In winter, cattle were fed on hay cut from meadows at midsummer.

To MAKE WINE, grapes were trampled underfoot in a big stone trough. The juice was collected, left to ferment, strained, then stored in jars.

SHEEP were sheared in early summer. The fleeces were washed, spun into thread and woven by women slaves. Most Romans' clothes were woolen.

THE ESTATE OWNER appointed an experienced farmer to run his estates and manage all the slaves. Estate managers might be loyal ex-slaves who had been given their freedom.

CLOSE to the villa, there was a farmhouse for the estate manager, barns, storerooms, workshops, stables, cattle-sheds, pigsties, a bakehouse, rooms where female slaves spun and wove wool and sleeping quarters for all the slaves.

wine-press room

kitchen

villa

oil storage jars

bakehouse

olive press

FACT: RICH ROMANS ATE FLAMINGOS AND PEACOCKS

RICH ROMANS liked to invite their friends to sumptuous banquets, with all kinds of expensive food. Often, they hired a master-chef to cook these special meals. Guests arrived in the late afternoon and spent all evening reclining on couches in the 'triclinium' (dining room). Romans considered seven to be the ideal number of guests. There were always three couches: one for family members and two for the guests.

Ordinary people ate cheaper and simpler food: bread, porridge, olives, onions, garlic, cheese, salt fish and fruit. This was a much healthier diet than that eaten by the wealthy.

A ROMAN butcher's stall. Pork was popular, although most Romans could not afford meat.

ROMAN cooking utensils. Knives and ladles were made of iron and serving dishes and cauldrons of pottery.

GRAIN was measured out in wooden pails. When it was scarce and expensive, poor citizens received free food from the state, so they and their families would not starve.

WINE was served at many meals. It was always mixed with water.

THERE were hundreds of bakers in Rome. They bought grain in bulk, ground it in a mill, then baked small, round loaves in a red-hot brick oven. They often added olives, onions and garlic to the dough – an early kind of pizza.

ROMAN slaves cooked on a raised open hearth with a charcoal fire burning underneath.

WHILE diners enjoyed their meal, they might be entertained by dancers, musicians or slaves doing tricks. Sometimes, the host recited poetry, or started a discussion about politics.

IT was bad manners to get sick at the table. But diners who overate (and many did) could be sick in a nearby room, the 'vomitorium'. There, a slave looked after them until they felt well enough to return to the dining-room.

ONLY rich families had a separate dining room. Poor people ate in their single room.

WEALTHY Romans liked to eat and drink from precious hand-made glass and silverware.

MOST ordinary Roman homes did not have an oven. (Because of the fire risk, apartment-dwellers were forbidden to light fires in their rooms.) So they bought ready-cooked meals (bean stew, meat and vegetable pie) from fast-food shops, or ate a cheap meal at the nearest tavern.

FAMILIES whose houses had gardens often built an outside dining-room where they could enjoy meals in hot weather.

Facts about Roman Food:

Guests at a dinner party brought their own napkins so they could take food home with them to eat next day.

Romans had one main meal a day – dinner, in the early evening. Breakfast and lunch were just snacks of bread and fruit.

A slave, the 'scissor', carved and served the meat.

Roman meals had three courses: gustus ('a taste' or first course); cena (main course); secunda mensa ('second table' or dessert).

Some rich Romans liked to eat foods such as flamingos stuffed with dates, sows' udders with sea urchins, peacocks, stuffed dormice (a squirrellike rodent), snails fattened in milk or roses in pastry.

FACT: MANY ROMAN ROADS ARE STILL IN USE

THE ROMANS were great architects and engineers. They built temples, palaces, huge sports arenas, underground drainage systems, aqueducts, roads and bridges. Many Roman roads are still in use today. The surfaces have been repaired, but the foundations have lasted two thousand years.

Roman roads were built by the army, because the army used them most, as routes for marching quickly across the empire to deal with any trouble in the conquered territories. Army surveyors marked out the course, as straight as the land allowed, then the soldiers dug trenches, rammed down foundation layers and laid the surface paving stones.

BUILDERS' tools:
1 Plumb-bob.
2 Dividers.
3 Folding foot-rule.
4 Trowel.

wooden framework around which arch will be built

surveyors

STONE arches were built round a wooden framework. Masons cut stones to fit and held them together with mortar. With all the stones in place, the frame was removed.

ROMAN ROADS were made up of several layers:
1 Chalk and sand base.
2 Big, tight-packed stones.
3 Sand, gravel, broken bricks.
4 Top layer of carefully shaped paving stones. There was a drainage ditch on each side.

Facts about Roman Roads:
Although Roman roads were excellent, journeys were often dangerous. Attacks and kidnappings by highwaymen were a particular problem.

The government organized a system of fast dispatch riders to carry urgent messages and money between outlying provinces and Rome, the capital city. It was called the 'cursus publicus'.

The Romans invented concrete, a mixture of volcanic ash, lime, gravel and water.

ON LONG JOURNEYS, rich Romans traveled in a four-wheeled carriage pulled by two heavy horses. The carriage had a cloth cover to protect passengers from sun, rain and snow.

stone blocks

FACT: GOVERNMENT JOBS WERE FOR MEN ONLY

'SPQR' (Senatus Populusque Romanum – the Senate and People of Rome). This proud symbol of the Roman state was carried by the army on its standards.

FROM 509 BC Rome was a republic. The government was run by consuls, senators and senior officials on behalf of the people of Rome. Citizens met and discussed policies in assemblies and could vote to choose officials. But, for centuries, only men from powerful patrician families were eligible for top government posts.

After 27 BC, Rome was ruled by emperors. Although called 'first among equals', they had almost unlimited power. Some, like Hadrian (AD 117-138) ruled well. Others, like Tiberius (AD 14-37), were brutal. A few, like Caligula (AD 37-41) and Nero (AD 54-68), were insane.

AUGUSTUS (27 BC-AD 14) was the first emperor of Rome. He changed many laws to hold on to power.

Facts about Roman Government and Laws:
The Romans kept a flock of noisy geese to guard the Capitol, the ancient government center of Rome.

People accused of crimes sometimes put ashes in their hair and turned up in court wearing old, dirty clothes, to try to win the jury's sympathy.

Crime was common in Rome. Many Romans kept guard dogs. Some houses had a sign outside, saying 'Cave Canem' (Beware of the dog).

SENATORS met to discuss policy and make laws. The Senate was most powerful in Republican times (509-27 BC).

CIVILIANS accused of a crime were tried by a jury. They employed a lawyer to argue their case in court – if they could afford his fees. The jury listened to the evidence then gave its verdict. The judge then passed sentence, according to the law.

NON-VIOLENT crimes, like debt or fraud, were punished by a fine and paying compensation to the victim.

EXILE or losing Roman citzen- ship were the sentences for more serious crimes. Major crimes were punished by slavery – in the mines or rowing a galley (below).

The Romans prided themselves on their laws. They made a great many, and frequently revised them to deal with problems as the empire grew. In the 1st century AD they made many new laws to deal with tensions in overcrowded Rome.

Roman courts were well organized and trials were usually fair. But Roman punishments for convicted criminals could be very severe.

MANY rich young men began their political careers working in the law-courts.

CRUCIFIXION was a horrible death, reserved for traitors and anyone who rebeled against Rome.

ARMY PUNISHMENTS were very harsh. Deserters were beaten to death by other soldiers and traitors were crucified.

FACT: ROMANS SPENT HOURS IN THE BATH

ROMAN MEN got up at dawn and finished work early in the afternoon. Then they had plenty of time for one of their favorite pastimes: spending hours at the baths. Friends and business colleagues met there, to talk and relax. The biggest public baths were like modern leisure centers, with sports facilities and places to eat. Some even had a library and art gallery, too.

The Romans also liked to be well-dressed. Slaves had to wear simple clothes, but rich nobles wore elegant robes.

Facts about Roman Clothes and Vanity:

The Romans laughed at baldness. So they invented mixtures, such as rats' dung and pepper, to try to cure it.

Roman women nourished their skin with a facepack of breadcrumbs mixed with cream.

Slave-girls captured in Germany had their long blonde hair cut off by slave-traders who sold it to make wigs for Roman women.

Roman men never wore trousers. Tribesmen like the Scythians (from south Russia) and the Celts (from Britain and France) wore them. But the Romans believed their own short-skirted tunics were more manly.

ROMAN women wore an under-tunic covered by a 'stola', a floor-length robe.

A MAN'S main item of clothing was his toga, a long, semi-circular cloak. Only Roman citizens could wear them. Men and boys over 14 wore plain white ones. Senators' togas had a purple border.

CHILDREN wore clothes like adults'. Boys also wore a bulla, a lucky charm.

WEALTHY Roman women wore lots of jewelry and make-up, strong perfume and elaborate hair-styles. They had specially trained slaves to help them dress, arrange their hair and make up their faces.

GOING to the barber was a painful experience. Roman knives were not very sharp and grazed the skin. Some men pulled out their beard and chest hair with tweezers, instead.

THERE were about 170 bathhouses in Rome in 25 BC. By AD 300, there were 900.

BATHERS undressed in the changing room.

THEN they played games, or did exercises.

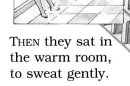

THEN they sat in the warm room, to sweat gently.

NEXT they went to the very hot steam room.

MAKE-UP KIT

make-up bowl

mirror

make-up tools

tweezers

spoons

strigils and oil container

A SLAVE scraped sweat and dirt off their skin. Now they had a choice – either the cold pool or a relaxing swim.

Facts about Roman Baths and Sewers:

The Baths of Caracalla, built AD 212-217, covered 32 acres.

Bathing was segregated. Women went to the baths in the morning, men in the afternoon.

Romans rarely used soap. Instead, they rubbed olive oil into their skin and scraped it off with an implement called a strigil. This cleaned well.

The largest Roman sewer, the Cloaca Maxima, was so big a horse and cart could be driven through it.

ROMAN CITIES had well-planned drains and fresh water supplies. Public toilets had seats side by side, and washable sponges on sticks to use like toilet paper.

FACT: ROMAN CROWDS WERE BLOODTHIRSTY

THE CITIZENS OF ROME enjoyed having fun – they liked music, plays, dancing and giving parties at home. But the most popular entertainments were gladiator fights, wild beast shows and chariot races, held in huge open-air arenas in the middle of Rome. The Romans found all these 'sports' very exciting. They were also dangerous and often very cruel. Gladiators were mostly specially trained prisoners and slaves, forced to fight until they died. Wild animals were trapped and brought to Rome – then brutally killed in the arena, just to amuse the crowds. So many wild animals were killed in these 'entertainments' that some species, for example the Asian lion, became extinct in lands close to Rome.

THE COLOSSEUM was built by Emperor Vespasian and his sons, Titus and Domitian, and opened in AD 80. It was Rome's largest amphitheater and could seat 50,000 spectators. It was used to stage gladiator fights and wild beast shows until it was closed by Emperor Honorius in AD 404-405. He was disgusted by the killing and cruelty. The Colosseum still stands, although it is in ruins.

The Colosseum in Rome, begun by the Emperor Vespasian.

seats for the poor, slaves and foreigners

wooden fence

women's seats

statues decorating outer walls

ROMAN stone carving showing two gladiators carrying long shields and wearing full armor fighting against a lion and a bear.

Facts about Roman Sports:

Roman gladiators were almost as famous as rock stars today – and also attracted many female fans.

Chariot races were probably the most dangerous Roman sport. Many charioteers and their horses died when chariots collided.

There were some women gladiators, although they mostly staged mock fights to win laughs. They were banned in AD 200.

WHEN a gladiator was defeated the emperor (or the senior official present) decided whether he should live or die. A 'thumbs-up' signal meant he could live; but if it was 'thumbs-down' he was put to death at once in front of the cheering crowd.

arena

FACT: MANY ROMAN SOLDIERS COULDN'T SPEAK LATIN

THE ROMAN PEOPLE spoke a language called Latin. The first Roman soldiers naturally spoke Latin, too. But, as the Roman Empire expanded beyond Italy, army recruits came from many different lands. They spoke their own local languages, and fought with local weapons such as bows and arrows and sling-shots.

At the beginning of a battle, cavalry on horseback charged towards the enemy, trying to frighten them away. Then all the other soldiers rushed towards them on foot, slashing at them with swords and spears.

A ROMAN legionary signed up with the army for 16 years' service.

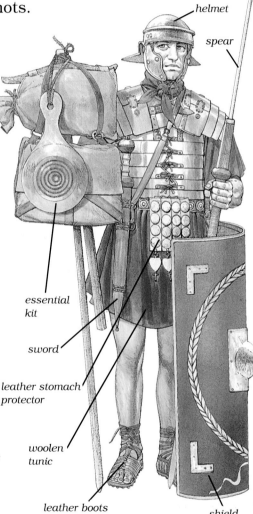

helmet

spear

essential kit

sword

leather stomach protector

woolen tunic

leather boots

shield

tent made of leather

AFTER a day's march the soldiers set up camp every night. Eight soldiers shared a tent. On campaign, they ate porridge, dry biscuits, bacon, cheese and wine.

SOLDIERS defending the frontiers lived in forts, mostly built to a grid design and surrounded by deep ditches and strong walls.

IT WAS the army's duty to protect the frontiers of the empire. If conquered peoples rebelled, troops had to move quickly to trouble spots. A soldier on the march carried his weapons, bedding, water-beaker, cooking pot and enough food to feed himself for three days.

Facts about Army Life:

Soldiers were expected to march 20 miles a day. They were not allowed to marry, but many had 'unofficial' families.

Letters from Roman soldiers in northern Britain survive. They complain of the cold and ask their families to send warm clothes. They also wore underclothes – the first Roman soldiers to do so – in their efforts to keep warm.

siege tower

onager

THE ROMAN ARMY was the best-trained, best-equipped and best-organized in the world. It was divided into legions, each with about 5,500 soldiers. The legion's commander was called a legate. He was assisted by six officers, called tribunes. As the Roman Empire expanded, local tribesmen were recruited to form cohorts. These auxiliary troops backed up the main army.

SOLDIERS injured in battle were cared for in well-equipped army hospitals. Many of the doctors were former slaves.

THE GOVERNMENT gave a 'triumph' to a victorious general. Troops and prisoners marched through the streets of Rome.

THE ROMANS excelled at siege warfare. They built many different types of war machine: onagers to hurl stones, battering rams to smash stonework and siege towers to help besiegers climb over walls. Few enemies were strong enough to survive an attack by the Roman army.

27

FACT: THE ROMANS BELIEVED IN GHOSTS

THE ROMANS worshiped many different gods and goddesses. Each one had special powers, to help, guide or protect worshipers who prayed to them, or who gave them offerings and sacrifices. Jupiter was king of the gods; he sent thunder and lightning. Mars was the god of war; he brought victory or defeat. Neptune was god of the sea; he sent shipwreck or a prosperous voyage. Venus was the beautiful goddess of love, and kindly Ceres made the crops and flowers grow.

Many Romans believed in ghosts and demons. They feared they might meet them flitting among the tombs that lined the Appian Way – one of the main roads leading out of Rome. They left offerings at graves to help unquiet spirits rest in peace.

During the 1st century AD, these traditional Roman beliefs began to change as the Roman people started to follow new religions from the Middle East: Mithraism and Christianity.

EVERY DAY, Roman families said prayers to the invisible spirits, the 'Lares and Penates', who protected their homes. On holy days, they also made offerings of food and flowers.

CARVING showing animals about to be sacrificed at a temple to please the gods.

Facts about Roman Religion:
Romans were very superstitious. Each year had a number of 'dies nefasti' (unlucky days) when the Senate did not meet and businesses and shops stayed shut.

The Romans believed being left-handed was unlucky. Today, 'sinister', the Latin word for 'left', is used to mean 'strange' or 'menacing'.

After an animal was sacrificed, priests inspected its liver and heart, believing they foretold the future.

THE CULT OF MITHRAS

The Persian god Mithras was popular with soldiers. He represented youth, strength and the victory of life over death. He was usually portrayed in statues and carvings as a strong young man killing a bull. Believing in Mithras helped soldiers feel strong and brave in battle.

Soldiers who worshiped Mithras took part in mysterious rituals, sometimes wearing masks or disguises and often in darkness and silence. Shrines dedicated to Mithras have been found in many Roman forts.

MARS was the god of war and battles. He was often portrayed in huge statues wearing a warrior's breast-plate and ceremonial plumed helmet (right) and carrying a tall spear.

VESTAL VIRGINS were priestesses recruited from the patrician families. It was their duty to tend the sacred flame (below) that burned on the Capitol in Rome. If it went out, disaster would follow.

ROMANS built magnificent temples as homes for gods and goddesses in the center of Rome and other cities in the empire. Temples were also built to honor dead emperors, who (for political reasons) were said to become gods after they died. Roman temples were copied from ancient Greek ones.

TEMPLES were built of marble with clay tile roofs.

GLOSSARY

Amphitheater Large, open-air arena, usually circular.

Aqueducts Raised channels, carrying fresh water over long distances. Aqueducts brought enormous quantities of water to the city of Rome from the mountains nearby.

Auxiliaries Soldiers recruited into the Roman army from non-Roman tribes living in the Roman Empire.

Bulla Protective charm worn round the neck by Roman boys until they were 14.

Cavalry Soldiers who fought on horseback.

Cohorts Units of auxiliary soliders, made up of either 480 or 800 men.

Colonnades Walkways with rows of columns on either side.

Consuls Leaders of the government in Republican Rome. Two were appointed every year.

Equites Romans of middle rank.

Galley A warship powered by oars. Usually rowed by slaves.

Insula (plural, **insulae**) Apartment block.

Legion Division of the Roman army.

Onager Wild donkey. Also the name o a Roman war-machine, which hurled stones at the enemy.

Patricians Top-ranking nobles.

Plebs (or **plebeians**) The ordinary people of Rome.

Scribe Someone trained to read and write, who used these skills to earn a living.

Senate Assembly of former top government officials. It advised on government policy and made new laws

Steppes Vast grass-covered plains.

Terracotta Type of clay that turns brick-red when fired (baked).

Triumph Ceremonial procession through the streets of Rome, ending in solemn sacrifices. Awarded as a great honor to successful generals.

Villa Grand country house.

INDEX